art

AND HOW IT WORKS

An introduction
to art for children

Written by Ann Kay
Senior editor Marie Greenwood
US editors Karyn Gerhard, Allison Singer
Senior designer Jim Green
Design assistant Xiao Lin
Senior picture researcher Myriam Mégharbi
Jacket designer Elle Ward
Jacket coordinator Francesca Young
Senior pre-producer Nikoleta Parasaki
Senior producer Isabell Schart
Managing editor Laura Gilbert
Managing art editor Diane Peyton Jones
Creative director Helen Senior
Publishing director Sarah Larter

First American Edition, 2018
Published in the United States by DK Publishing
345 Hudson Street, New York, New York 10014

Copyright © 2018 Dorling Kindersley Limited
DK, a Division of Penguin Random House LLC
18 19 20 21 22 10 9 8 7 6 5 4 3 2 1
001–305914–Nov/2018

A catalog record for this book
is available from the Library of Congress.
ISBN: 978-1-4654-6802-4

DK books are available at special discounts when purchased
in bulk for sales promotions, premiums, fund-raising, or
educational use. For details, contact: DK Publishing Special
Markets, 345 Hudson Street, New York, New York 10014
SpecialSales@dk.com

Printed and bound in China

A WORLD OF IDEAS:
SEE ALL THERE IS TO KNOW

www.dk.com

Contents

Foreword

When I was only four years old, I announced to my family, "When I grow up, I am going to be an artist. I am going to write stories and draw pictures for books—and sing and tap dance on the stage."

I was excited to start going to school. My older brother had told me there was an art teacher who gave lessons to each grade. He failed to tell me, however, that the kindergarten and first grade were not included. You can probably imagine my disappointment and outrage when I found this out. "But, I'M going to be an ARTIST when I grow up," I'd protest. "I NEED those art lessons!"

I would gaze with awe when Mrs. Beulah Bowers walked down the hallway in her long blue artist's smock. I had heard on the playground that Mrs. Bowers showed the classes how to draw things. When I finally got to second grade, I found out this was true. We drew pilgrims and turkeys for Thanksgiving, trees and stars for Christmas, and roses and violets for Valentine's Day.

Mrs. Bowers held a "Sketchbook Contest" for the fourth, fifth, and sixth grades each year. To enter, you had to keep a sketchbook. In the spring, prizes for the best ones would be awarded! When I reached fourth grade, I entered the contest for the first time.

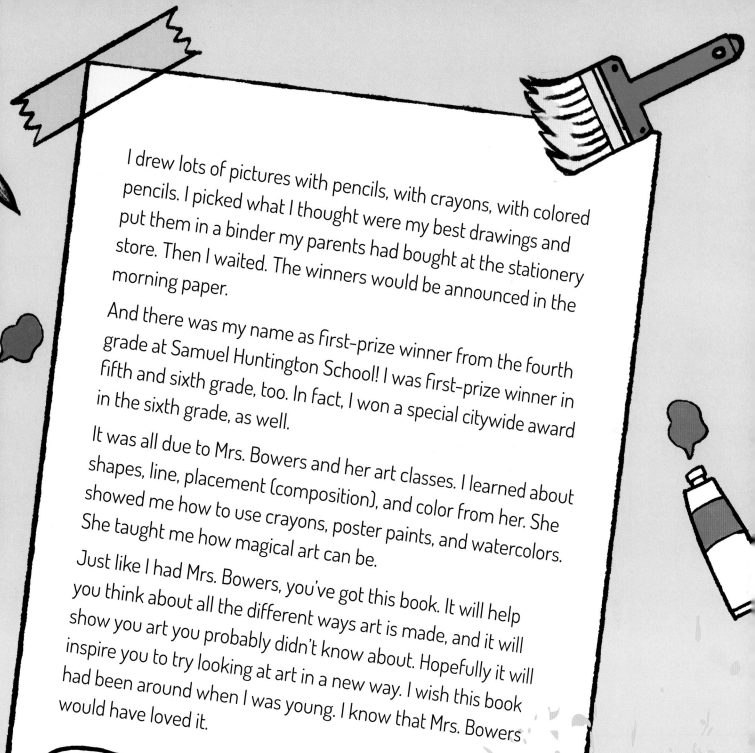

I drew lots of pictures with pencils, with crayons, with colored pencils. I picked what I thought were my best drawings and put them in a binder my parents had bought at the stationery store. Then I waited. The winners would be announced in the morning paper.

And there was my name as first-prize winner from the fourth grade at Samuel Huntington School! I was first-prize winner in fifth and sixth grade, too. In fact, I won a special citywide award in the sixth grade, as well.

It was all due to Mrs. Bowers and her art classes. I learned about shapes, line, placement (composition), and color from her. She showed me how to use crayons, poster paints, and watercolors. She taught me how magical art can be.

Just like I had Mrs. Bowers, you've got this book. It will help you think about all the different ways art is made, and it will show you art you probably didn't know about. Hopefully it will inspire you to try looking at art in a new way. I wish this book had been around when I was young. I know that Mrs. Bowers would have loved it.

Tomie dePaola

This book is packed with all kinds of exciting art, with questions to get you thinking. You'll find the answers in the back. Some questions don't have a right or wrong answer—they just might make you think!

Lines and shapes

How you use lines and shapes is very important in art.

Lines might be thick or thin, straight or curved. Shapes can be an outline, or solid if they are colored in. They can be geometrical, like a rectangle, or rounded and freer, like a fluffy cloud. Artists might use jagged lines to create an angry mood, or draw curvy shapes for a calm feeling.

Circle

Horizontal lines

Vertical lines

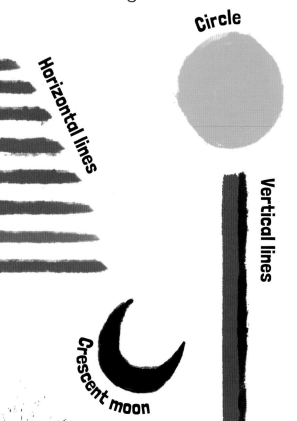

Crescent moon

SPOT IT!

Can you see the ear on the tree?

V shapes that look like birds

Look at the lines and shapes on these pages.
Can you find them in the painting?

▼ *The Tilled Field, Joan Miró, 1923–24*

See also

Find out about another very important feature of art—using color—on pages 8–9.

Taillike shape

Circle with dot

Diagonal lines

Real and unreal

Here, Spanish artist Joan Miró has painted his family's farm, which he loved. Some shapes are realistic, like the animals, but others seem made-up! Can you see an animal with a shell in the picture?

Spiral

Leaf shape

Wavy lines

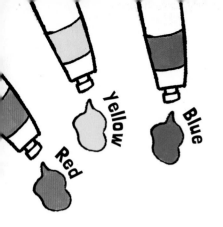

Yellow
Blue
Red

Using color

Artists need to understand how colors work to make great paintings.

Some artists try to make things exactly the same color as they are in real life. Others don't think this is so important, so they use colors to express how they feel or their ideas instead.

Primary colors

The three primary paint colors are red, yellow, and blue. You use these to make all other colors.

If colors are side by side on the wheel, they blend more with each other.

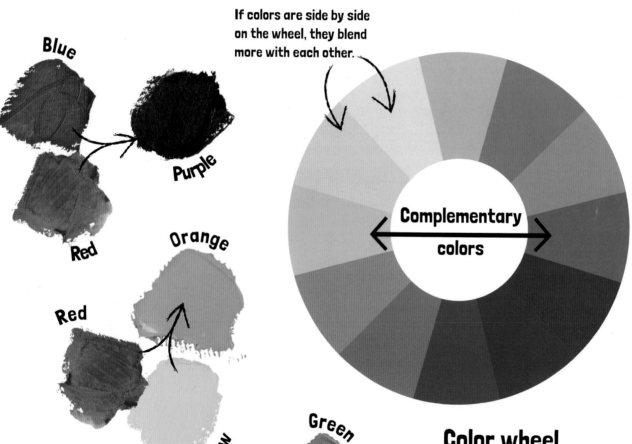

Blue

Red

Purple

Orange

Red

Yellow

Green

Yellow

Blue

Complementary colors

Mixing colors

Purple, orange, and green are the main colors you get when you mix primary colors together.

Color wheel

Paint colors can be arranged in a wheel. Opposite colors on the wheel, like orange and blue, are "complementary colors." This means they contrast with each other. If you put them side by side they are strong and bold.

Which two of these three pairs of complementary colors can you see in this painting?

▲ *Cows (Painting with Cows I), Franz Marc, 1913*

Using complementary colors

In this picture, German artist Franz Marc has made bold, colorful patterns. Where he has put one complementary color next to another, they both really stand out! Where his colors are side by side on the color wheel, like his greens and blue-greens, they blend together more calmly.

See also
Find out about other artists who loved to use bold colors on pages 64–65 and 78–79.

First artists

Throughout history, people have made pictures.

Stone Age people lived thousands of years ago. They painted pictures that described their lives on the walls of caves, just as you might draw a picture now and stick it on the wall. Their art used lots of black, red, brown, and yellow, and often showed animals.

Cave paintings

Early artists painted colorful scenes with natural materials. They used dirt, charcoal, powdered rock, and liquid to make paints. Paint was smeared, brushed, or dabbed onto cave walls with hands, brushes, and leather pads.

A red, yellow, or brown mineral called ocher was ground into a powder and used to make paint.

Horsehair brush for a heavy coat of paint

Shell used as a palette

Charcoal was used to add black.

Leather pad filled with moss

Tools

Anything that could be found easily, such as twigs and moss, was used for painting. A good brush might have been made by attaching animal hair or feathers to a large twig.

Goose feather paintbrush for light coats

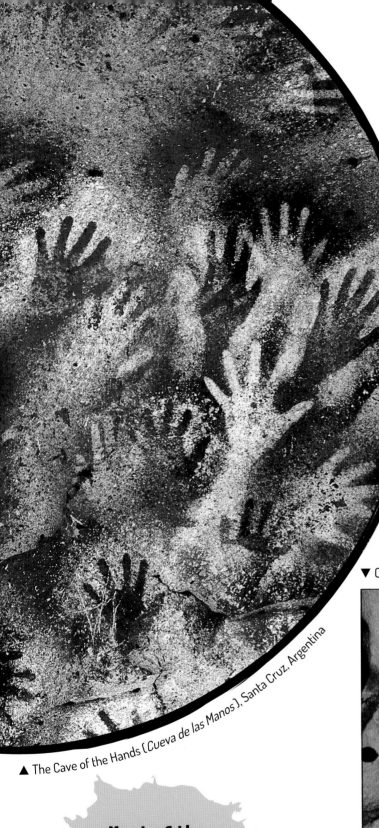

▲ The Cave of the Hands (*Cueva de las Manos*), Santa Cruz, Argentina

See also
A favorite subject for artists is animals. See pages 12 and 13 for more animal pictures.

Some early artists placed their hands on a wall and blew paint on them.

Spray paint

Early people often did spray painting! They blew paint through a hollow bird bone. It was like blowing paint through a straw. Can you think of ways to make hand paintings with your hands?

▼ Cave painting, Lascaux, Dordogne, France

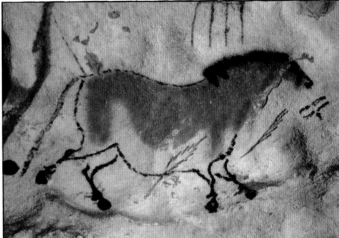

Most of the hands in this cave are left hands. Can you guess why?

Animal pictures

Some well-known cave paintings are found in Lascaux, in southwest France. Many of the paintings show animals that people hunted for food. Artists knew the animals well and drew them accurately. Can you tell what animal is shown here?

Blue horse

German artist Franz Marc chose bright colors and bold shapes to show what it felt like to be a horse, rather than show what a horse looks like in real life.

▼ *Zebra*, Victor Vasarely, c.1938

Fun with stripes

This Hungarian–French artist has made a zebra puzzle! It's hard to see where one zebra ends and the other begins.

Painting horses

Horses have been a subject in art since the time of cave paintings.

People have always loved horses for being both beautiful and useful animals. If you look at these pictures, you can see how artists have painted horses using all kinds of styles, colors, and techniques.

Which of these pictures of horses is your favorite?

▼ *Whistlejacket*, George Stubbs, **c.1762**

▼ *Horse and Willow*, Utagawa Kunisada, **1830s**

Galloping horse

This Japanese artist was famous for making popular prints. His bold style uses very few brushstrokes to create a horse that looks like it's moving.

The horse is shown life-size. The painting is more than twice the height of a nine-year-old child! It is 97 x 115 in (246 x 292 cm).

Portrait of a horse

This picture of a racehorse called Whistlejacket was painted by British artist George Stubbs. The picture is incredibly lifelike and detailed.

The artist left the background plain. This is so we just focus on the horse and nothing else.

See also

You can see a cave painting of a horse on page 11 and more of Victor Vasarely's art on page 84.

Wall art

▼ Tomb of Nefertari, Valley of the Queens, Thebes, Egypt, c.1200s BCE

SPOT IT!
See how the queen's body is shown from the front, but her head from the side.

You don't need canvas or paper to paint on—a wall will do!

People have been creating art on walls ever since the first cave painters. Artists might paint inside tombs or in buildings where people worship. Other artists paint in city streets for everyone to see and share.

Egyptian tomb painting

The Ancient Egyptians were skilled artists. They covered walls with plaster and painted on that. This painting is in the tomb of Queen Nefertari. The Egyptians believed their paintings helped people to go to a happy place after they had died.

▼ Dome of the Rock, Jerusalem, Middle East

Islamic mosaic

This is an outside wall of a shrine (a place of worship) in Jerusalem. This ancient shrine is very important to Muslims, who follow Islam. Its walls are decorated in beautifully patterned mosaics made from tiles.

Look at the boy's face—how do you think he's feeling?

Street art, Malaysia

Today, many people paint words or pictures on walls in towns and cities. This is called graffiti. This wall painting is by Lithuanian artist Ernest Zacharevic. The picture is based on two children who are brother and sister.

SPOT IT!
Is the bicycle painted on the wall, too?

▲ *Little Children on a Bicycle*, Ernest Zacharevic, George Town, Penang, Malaysia, **2012**

▲ *Untitled*, Thierry Noir, East Side Gallery, Berlin, Germany, **c.1990**

See also
You can find out more about painting on plaster on pages 18–19 and painting gods on pages 16–17.

Comic wall art, Germany

French artist Thierry Noir painted colorful, comic characters on part of the Berlin Wall, in Germany. This wall once divided Berlin into East and West for political reasons. Today, this piece of wall is in a huge outdoor art gallery in Berlin.

Gods and myths

Since early times, gods and myths have been important in art.

Artists have found many imaginative ways of showing these invisible, spiritual worlds. Art can help explain religion and myths to people. Often signs, or symbols, are used in religious art.

▶ Ancient Greek vase, artist unknown, 540–530 BCE

▼ Chinese painted silk banner, artist unknown, c.851–900

The lady is supported on clouds.

Greek legends

Ancient Greek pottery often had black pictures painted onto brightly colored clay. This vase shows the god Heracles doing one of his "12 labors," or tasks. Here, Heracles is throwing a boar on top of a king.

Chinese Buddhism

This scene is painted on silk. A Buddhist holy person is on the left. He is guiding the lady on the right to the Buddhist "Pure Land." The land is shown by the Chinese buildings in the top left of the painting.

See also

Find out about gold in religious art on page 22 and more about symbols on pages 74–75.

Aboriginal dreamtime

Australian Aboriginal people have a set of beliefs about how the world was created. This is called the Dreamtime. Christine Napanangka Michaels is an Aboriginal artist who uses bright colors to show joyful Dreaming.

▼ *Lappi-Lappi-Dreaming*, Christine Napanangka Michaels, 2016

▲ *The Baptism of Christ*, Piero della Francesca, **1450s**

SPOT IT!
Can you see how the dove looks like one of the clouds?

Artists made egg tempera by mixing different pigment colors with egg yolk. It dried very quickly and lasted a long time.

Christian art

Religious art is often full of symbols. In this painting, can you see the dove hovering over the man in the middle of the painting? This man is Christ, and the dove is a Christian symbol of peace. The painting was created using egg tempera paint, made from egg yolk.

▼ *Mona Lisa*, Leonardo da Vinci, c.1503–19

Woman of mystery

This picture was painted by Italian artist Leonardo da Vinci, one of the most important figures of the Renaissance. The painting is famous for being of an unknown woman who has eyes that follow you!

UP CLOSE! As you walk past, you feel her eyes looking straight at you.

The Renaissance was a period in history when exciting things happened in art!

Renaissance

The Renaissance was a time in history in the 1400s and 1500s when people had new ideas about the world, including art. "Renaissance" means "rebirth"— when something is born again. This was used because ideas from Ancient Greece and Rome came back into fashion.

The angle of the floor going back makes the space seem real.

Space and light

Renaissance artists showed space and light in a new way to make pictures look real, not flat. This is called "perspective." They used a type of wall painting called fresco, as Italian artist Fra Angelico has here. Fresco is painting onto wet plaster. When it dries, the painting becomes part of the wall.

Sketching faces

Some Renaissance artists made lots of sketches of people. They wanted to draw the human body accurately, but also wanted people to look beautiful. Italian artist Michelangelo made this drawing using red chalk. Some parts are lightly sketched in, while others are more detailed. Look at the woman's fine and delicate eyelashes!

It's not all realistic, though. If these figures stood up, they would bang their heads!

The light and shadow on the columns and arches makes them seem like actual solid objects.

▲ *The Annunciation*, Fra Angelico, **c.1440**

See also

Find out more about space and perspective on pages 20–21 and page 33.

Near and far

How do you show objects and distances on a flat surface?

Most paintings are flat surfaces. But artists are often trying to show things that aren't flat—objects, such as trees, that might be close up or off in the distance. So they use tricks to make you think you are seeing real objects either near to you or far away. This is called perspective.

Painting the distant sky pale blue helps to make it seem far away, because things in the distance look bluish in real life.

The trees also form lines going back to the vanishing point.

Vanishing point

Horizon line

Where the land meets the sky is called the horizon.

The road leads back to the vanishing point.

How to show distance

To show distance, artists such as Hobbema base their pictures on some simple lines, like the ones shown here. The place where the road meets the horizon is called the vanishing point.

See also

Find out how Renaissance artists invented using lines with a vanishing point on pages 18–19.

The head of the man walking toward us is the same level as our eye level when looking at the picture. That's why we feel we are walking toward him!

Getting smaller and smaller ...

In real life, objects that are nearer to us seem larger than those farther away. In this Dutch painting, the road gets narrower as it goes back. The people at the far end of the road are smaller than the man walking toward us, so we feel like we are looking into the distance.

SPOT IT!
Can you see the dog on the road?

Gold

Using gold adds magic to paintings! Gold means luxury, royalty, beauty, decoration, and holiness.

Gold is a precious metal, so it is a very special kind of color to use in art. Artists have used it to show important religious people, as well as kings and queens. Because of its beauty, it is also perfect for creating lovely decorative patterns.

Various tools and brushes are needed to work with gold leaf.

A gold background instead of sky or a wall makes the picture "otherworldly," or holy.

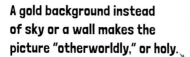
Gold coin

Gold leaf

Making gold

Gold leaf means sheets of gold. Artists often made these by beating gold coins into very thin sheets. They also used ground-up gold to make gold paint, and even sprinkled gold dust over their work.

▶ "The Wilton Diptych," artist unknown, c.1395–99

Heavenly gold

This painting is one half of a diptych, which is a piece of art in two parts. The figure kneeling is Richard II, King of England, 1377–99. Behind him are three saints. Medieval artists loved gold. In candlelit churches, glimmering gold made art seem heavenly and holy.

Adele Bloch-Bauer I, Gustav Klimt, 1907

SPOT IT!

What other precious metal can you see in the picture?

Can you see the Ancient Egyptian-style eyes on the painting?

Golden lady

This beautiful portrait of a wealthy woman is covered in glowing gold leaf. It was made by Austrian artist Gustav Klimt. The woman is actually sitting on a chair, but the modern style makes the picture look like a big abstract pattern. All the gold makes this woman seem like a goddess.

See also

See other examples of religious art on pages 16–17 and see more patterns on pages 26–27.

Oil painting

How many ways can you paint a red hat?

Lots of ways—if you use oil paint! It is great for thick or thin coats, bold strokes, or tiny details. Also, it dries slowly. So there's time to add to it, make changes, and fix mistakes while the paint is still wet.

See also

Discover more about painting techniques on pages 54–55. See another painting by van Eyck on page 74.

The dark background and bright red turban make us concentrate on the man's face.

▼ *Portrait of Gauguin*, Vincent van Gogh, **1888**

▼ *Portrait of a Man*, Jan van Eyck, **1433**

Thick

Dutch painter van Gogh was an expressive artist, which means he showed his feelings through the way he painted. You can see this in his painting of French artist Paul Gauguin. Van Gogh has painted the red hat with thick, bold strokes.

Fine

Jan van Eyck came from Maaseik, a town now in Belgium. He was very clever with oil paint. See how he used oils to paint fine details like the man's eyes and the hat's folds.

How to make oil paint

Oil paint is made by mixing ground-up pigment with oil. Linseed oil is often used for this. It is made by squeezing the seeds of the flax plant.

SPOT IT!

In Vermeer's painting, can you see the hat's red shadow across the girl's face?

Flax plant with seed pods

Flax seeds **Linseed oil** **Pigment**

▼ *Girl with the Red Hat*, Johannes Vermeer, **c.1665–66**

▼ *Young Girl in a Red Hat*, Edvard Munch, **c.1900**

Glaze

A glaze is a see-through layer on top of the paint that changes how it looks. Dutch painter Johannes Vermeer made this hat glow by painting a ruby glaze over a darker red.

Loose

Norwegian artist Edvard Munch wanted to show feelings in his art. He used oils to paint loosely and freely. See how the background color overlaps the edge of the hat. How do you think this girl is feeling?

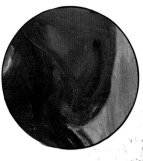

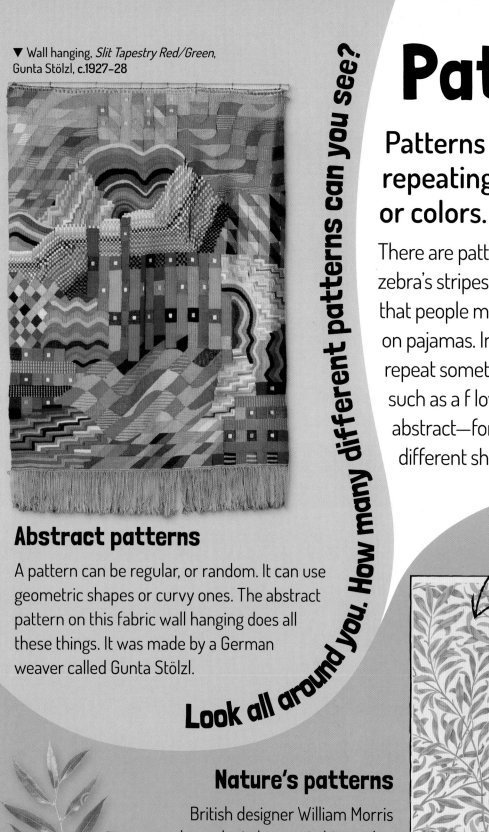

▼ Wall hanging, *Slit Tapestry Red/Green*, Gunta Stölzl, c.1927–28

How many different patterns can you see? Look all around you.

Patterns

Patterns are made by repeating shapes, lines, or colors.

There are patterns in nature, like a zebra's stripes. There are also patterns that people make, such as the stripes on pajamas. In art, a pattern might repeat something you recognize, such as a f lower. Or it might be abstract—for example, it might show different shades of the same color.

Abstract patterns

A pattern can be regular, or random. It can use geometric shapes or curvy ones. The abstract pattern on this fabric wall hanging does all these things. It was made by a German weaver called Gunta Stölzl.

The pattern is carefully repeated, but it also looks very free and natural.

Nature's patterns

British designer William Morris drew plants he saw in his garden or on walks in the country. He made wallpapers and fabrics with repeating natural patterns—like this one based on willow branches.

Willow branch

▲ *Willow Bough*, wallpaper, William Morris, 1887

Crazy patterns

This abstract picture by French artist
Auguste Herbin looks a little bit like a pattern—
but do you think it is? It's full of geometric
shapes. Some are repeated and some
aren't. It also repeats similar colors.

See also
There are more
patterns on
pages 84–85.

Sculpture

Sculptures have been made for thousands of years.

They are three-dimensional (3-D) objects. This means they have length, width, and depth, rather than being flat, like paintings. Sculptures are often carved out of wood or stone, or cast (molded) from metal. Sculptures can also be shaped from lots of other materials.

Bronze

This Ancient Greek statue has been cast in bronze. Bronze is made from the metals copper and tin. With casting, hot liquid bronze is poured into a mold (the shape of the statue). When the bronze cools, it hardens.

▼ Bronze statue of Zeus, Greece, c.460 BCE

SPOT IT!
Can you see how detailed the hair curls and beard are?

▲ *Mother and Child*, Barbara Hepworth, 1934

Stone

British sculptor Barbara Hepworth carved this sculpture from pink limestone. She liked simple, strong shapes that were often abstract. This means they did not look like the real thing. Do you think the sculpture looks like a mother and child?

▲ *Maman*, Louise Bourgeois, 1999

Chisel

Hammer

The spider is 365 in (927 cm) high—about seven times the height of an eight-year-old child!

Steel

French-American artist Louise Bourgeois designed this huge steel spider. Its title, *Maman*, means "Mom" in French. The artist's mother worked as a weaver, a job that is like a spider weaving its webs! Does it have the same number of legs as a real spider?

See also
Look at some other artworks of people on pages 38–39 and 48–49.

Mallet

▲ Haida Indian totem pole, Canada

Woodworking chisel

Wood

This is the top of a totem pole. Poles like this represent Native American history and culture. They are usually carved from huge trees and often look like animals. This is an eagle, a symbol of courage.

The pink stone gives a feeling of the love and warmth between a mother and child.

▼ *The Gleaners*, Jean-François Millet, 1857

▼ *Portrait of a Woman of the Hofer Family*, artist unknown, **c.1470**

GEBORNE HOFERIN.

People at work

This painting shows women collecting scraps of corn. In the mid-1800s, many people were shocked that anyone might paint realistic working lives. They thought art ought to be beautiful and show people who were rich or important, or show religious or legendary figures.

SPOT IT!

Can you see the tiny forget-me-not flowers on the painting?

Realistic art

Art can look a lot like real life!

Some artists want to make lifelike art. Pictures may be so real that they look like photos. "Realism" when used in art history means paintings from the mid-1800s that showed everyday life rather than grand scenes.

Early photo-realism

Has a tiny insect landed on this painting? Or is it painted on? Some artists made realistic art to show off their skills. *Trompe-l'oeil* is French for "tricks the eye." It is often used to mean things in art that fool us into thinking they are real and not painted.

New photo-realism

Is this a blurry photo? No—it's an oil painting! German artist Gerhard Richter often makes art that looks like photos. This painting shows his daughter, Betty, and was inspired by a photo of her. She is turning away from us. It makes us curious to know more about her.

▼ *Children Playing Game,* Duane Hanson, 1979

Realistic sculpture

Look closely. Amazingly, these aren't real children! American artist Duane Hanson made sculptures of ordinary American people doing ordinary things. They are made of plastic but wear real clothes. Do you think this is boring or interesting?

See also
Explore art that really is photographic on pages 50–51, and everyday things on pages 80–81.

In Ancient Greece, an artist called Zeuxis painted some grapes that looked so real, birds tried to eat them!

▲ *Betty,* Gerhard Richter, 1988

Home life

From the 1600s, scenes showing people at home, doing everyday things, became popular.

In Holland, artists such as Johannes Vermeer painted homey scenes of both rich and poor people. Today, artists across the world create scenes of everyday life.

The brilliant blue of the milkmaid's skirt was painted with ultramarine (pigment made from lapis lazuli).

Ultramarine

Servant's work

Here a milkmaid is quietly pouring milk. Vermeer has made a calm, peaceful scene out of an ordinary activity. See how hard she is concentrating. This makes us look closely, too.

Everyday life

Swedish artist Carl Larsson made happy pictures of his family's daily life at home. Here, his youngest son Esbjörn is staring out of the window instead of doing his homework. Can you see the man reflected in the mirror? That's Carl himself!

◀ *Esbjörn Doing His Homework*, Carl Larsson, 1912

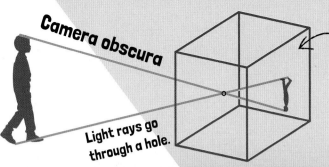

Camera obscura

Light rays go through a hole.

Vermeer probably used a "camera obscura" to help him plan pictures. This was a simple camera with no film. If you pointed it at something, it made an upside-down image inside. Vermeer would have traced around the image and used it (the right way around) in his art.

You can see the girl's reflection in the mirror.

The girl is playing an expensive keyboard instrument called a virginal.

▼ *The Music Lesson*, Johannes Vermeer, c.1662–64

SPOT IT!

Can you see a little bit of a painter's easel reflected in the mirror? The artist is saying "I painted this!"

Wealthy home

We know this is a wealthy home because of the people's clothes and the furniture in the room. The way the painting is arranged, with the checkered floor tiles getting smaller and smaller, draws us toward the girl. This is called using perspective.

See also

See more ultramarine on pages 62–63 and learn more about perspective in art on pages 20–21.

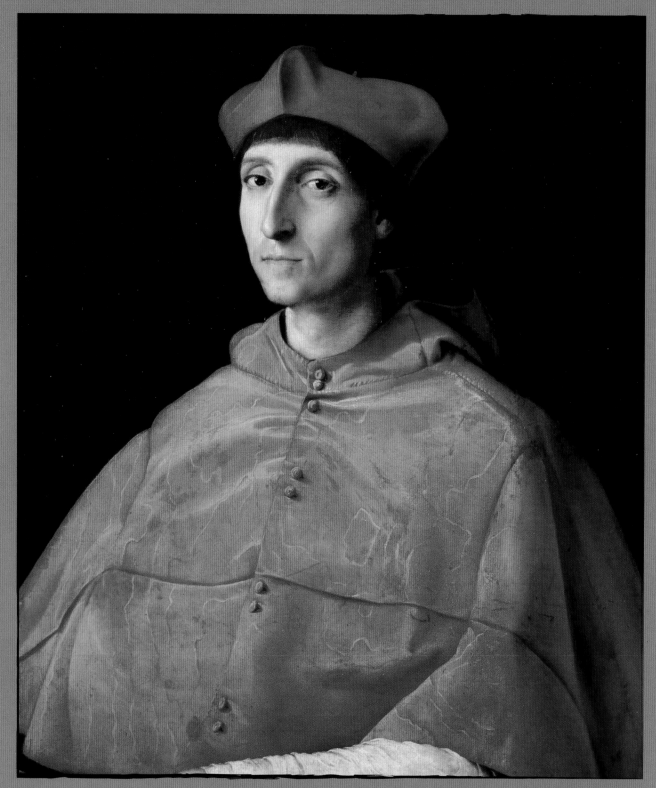

▲ *The Cardinal*, Raphael, 1510–11

SPOT IT!

Can you see how the artist uses lighter and darker shades of red to show folds in the cardinal's robe?

The color of power

Here the Italian artist Raphael has painted a cardinal, although no one is certain which one. Cardinals were powerful church officials in Raphael's time and were often very strict. This picture focuses on the red robes. The bright figure shines out of a dark background, making him seem even more powerful.

Red

Red is the color of fire, blood, danger, and love. It is linked with strong feelings and power.

Red has all kinds of meanings in both art and nature. Red roses are a symbol of love. A red chili is very spicy and hot to eat. A bright-red ladybug shouts danger, as it is poisonous to eat!

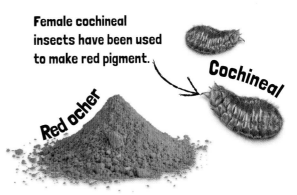

Female cochineal insects have been used to make red pigment.

Cochineal

Red ocher

Making red

Throughout history, artists have used many different red pigments. Carmine is made from dried cochineal insects, while red ocher is a powdered mineral.

Shades of red

How many different shades of red can you see when you look at the things around you? Shades include a deep red called crimson, and scarlet, which is a bright red. You might blush and turn scarlet when you're embarrassed! Pink is a paler shade of red. Think of a subject you would like to paint that uses red. Which shades would you use?

Seeing the color red can make your heart beat faster!

Chilies

Rose

Ladybug

See also

Turn to page 10 to learn more about ocher and how the first artists used it.

Light and shadow

Many artists are clever at using light and shadow to make beautiful, dramatic, or realistic art.

If you look at this painting, can you see how using dark shadows and bright light together helps give a sense of drama? This use of light and shadow in a painting is called *chiaroscuro*, which is Italian for "bright-dark."

See also

Learn more about symbols on pages 16–17 and 74–75.

Light effects

Can you see how light hits this flask of water?

What might make us think that the men on either side of Christ have discovered something amazing?

Shadows and symbols

This painting is by Italian artist Caravaggio. It shows Christ telling two disciples (followers) who didn't recognize him at first who he really is. Contrasting lighting makes this moment special and sacred.

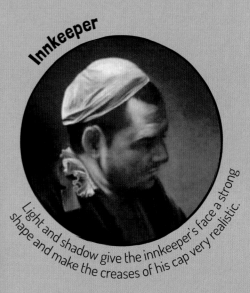

Innkeeper

Light and shadow give the innkeeper's face a strong shape and make the creases of his cap very realistic.

Shadowy halo

The innkeeper casts a shadow behind Christ. Its shape is like a halo (a ring above a holy person's head).

Basket of fruit

This basket looks as if it's about to fall off the table!

▲ *The Supper at Emmaus*, Caravaggio, 1601

Painting people

There are all kinds of different ways of showing people in art.

A picture that concentrates on showing a person and not much else is called a portrait. Some portraits tell us about people's lives by showing them doing something. People in portraits might look quite stiff and posed or very natural and normal.

SPOT IT!

The girl's left hand seems to point at herself, inviting us to look at her.

A girl

Many portraits just show the face and the top of the body. In this portrait, by Dutch artist Rembrandt, the girl is shown leaning out of a window. See how she seems to be asking us to come into her world.

▶ *Girl at a Window*, Rembrandt Harmensz. van Rijn, 1645

▼ *The Bus*, Frida Kahlo, 1929

A group

All kinds of different people are shown riding on this Mexican bus—just like you often find when you get on a bus or train. The woman on the far right might be the artist Frida Kahlo herself. She painted many self-portraits.

▼ *My Parents*, David Hockney, 1977

A couple

Here, British artist David Hockney has painted his parents. His mom sits straight, looking out. His dad is busy reading a book. Can you see the painting reflected in the mirror? You will find it on page 17!

See also

See some self-portraits on pages 48–49 and some photographic portraits on pages 50–51.

Landscape

Landscape art shows all kinds of outdoor scenes in nature, from green fields to snowy mountains.

In the 1800s, landscape pictures became very popular. Artists began to paint nature for its own sake, not just as a background. Some painted restful, everyday scenes. Others showed how powerful nature could be.

Constable made many studies of clouds. Can you tell what the weather is like from the clouds?

SPOT IT!
Can you see how Constable has used white paint to make the water sparkle?

▲ *The Hay Wain*, John Constable, 1821

Living in nature

The "hay wain" in this picture's title was a cart for carrying hay. British artist Constable has painted a typical summer day in the English countryside. This scene shows the area where he grew up.

See also

There's another artist who shows light on water on pages 58–59.

Looking at nature

German artist Caspar David Friedrich painted this exciting, dramatic landscape of swirling mists and peaks stretching on and on forever. By putting a figure with his back to us, we are seeing what he sees.

▲ *Wanderer above a Sea of Fog*, Caspar David Friedrich, c.1818

Delicate detail

Yun Shouping was a Chinese painter who created beautiful ink and watercolor pictures of flowers with delicate brushstrokes. He liked bright colors, and showed detail by using washes of color rather than lots of tiny lines.

Using fine washes gives a very natural effect.

Watercolor

Watercolor paintings are often done on paper.

Watercolor paint is colored pigment mixed with water. With this type of paint you can create "washes" (broad sweeps) of thin, see-through color.

▲ *Untitled* ("First Abstract Watercolor"), Wassily Kandinsky, c.1913

Watercolor goes well with ink and pencil, making lively shapes that seem to move around.

Mixed materials

Here, Russian artist Wassily Kandinsky uses watercolor with ink and pencil. Using different materials and paints together in a painting is called "mixed media."

Just add water to the paint!

Showing light

Watercolor is good for showing light because the thin paint lets the white paper show through. Or you can leave parts of white paper unpainted. British painter Eric Ravilious has done that here.

▼ *New Year Snow*, Eric Ravilious, 1935

Unpainted white paper gives the effect of light on the hills.

Wet-on-wet colors are mixed on the paper, not on the palette.

See also

Discover more about painting techniques on pages 24–25 and 54–55.

Wet on wet

"Wet on wet" is when you paint watercolor on top of wet paper or on top of another layer of wet paint. German artist August Macke does it here to create bold, glowing color. Can you see the woman mentioned in the picture's title?

▲ *Woman with a Yellow Jacket*, August Macke, 1913

Fall leaf

Colors of nature

Discover all kinds of earthy shades by looking at plants and animals. Leaves often turn brown in the fall, but some are red-brown or golden brown. You might spot orange lichen (like tiny plants) on a rock or see a moth flutter past showing its shades of brown.

Atlas moth

Lichen on a rock

Earth

Earthy colors are like the earth under our feet. They include the warm browns and rich yellows and oranges of soil, wood, and rocks. They are perfect for painting nature and country life, warm light, shade, the fall season, and skin tones.

Making earth colors

Painters have special names for the earthy pigments they use. The main ones include ochers, siennas, and umbers. Iron oxide is a major mineral in these colors.

See also

Find out more about earthy colours on page 10 and light and shade on pages 36–7.

Adding "burnt" to a pigment such as umber means it has been heated to make a richer color.

Iron oxide

Burnt umber

Browns and deep yellows and oranges are restful and blend together.

Special shades

Some people may find earthy colors a bit dull, but artists in the 1600s loved them. This is when Spanish artist Velázquez lived. In this painting, he uses earthy tones to tell us that he is showing an ordinary, everyday scene. But his rich shades and lovely light effects make the scene seem special.

▲ *The Waterseller of Seville*, Diego Velázquez, c.1620

Arranging nature

A picture made from a careful arrangement of things, such as fruit and flowers, is called a still life.

You can use other objects in a still-life picture, too—such as pretty jugs or plates. While the main things in the picture are not breathing and moving, you might find the odd creature creeping in, too!

See also

There are still lifes in the picture on pages 36–37. Learn about complementary colors on pages 8–9.

Squash

Peach

Wheat

Fly

The red plums and green grapes look colorful next to each other because green and red are complementary colors.

Corn

Birds' eggs

Can you see all these objects in the painting?

Grapes

▶ *Still Life with Fruit and Insects, Rachel Ruysch, 1711*

Butterfly

Snail

Still life and real life

Those juicy peaches look so real, it feels like you could just reach out and grab one! Rachel Ruysch was a Dutch artist who painted amazingly detailed still-life pictures. Paintings like this were very popular in her time.

Lizard

Beetle

Plum

Painting yourself

Some artists are famous for making many self-portraits—such as Paul Gauguin, who is shown here.

▼ 1. *Self-Portrait*, c.1875–77

▼ 2. *Self-Portrait with Portrait of Émile Bernard (Les Misérables)*, 1888

▼ 3. *Self-Portrait*, 1889

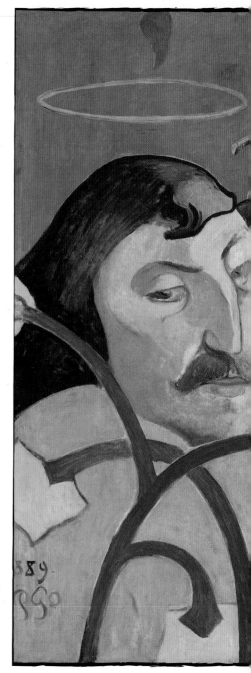

A picture that an artist makes of themselves is called a self-portrait. A self-portrait often tells us a lot about what was happening in an artist's life or how they felt when they painted it. The objects included in the painting may tell us something about the person, too.

SPOT IT!

Can you see which picture has another portrait in it?

Paul Gauguin

Paul Gauguin lived an interesting life and he helped to create modern art. Here are just some of his self-portraits. When you put self-portraits from different times in an artist's life together, it tells a story in paint about them.

▼ 4. *Self-Portrait with a Palette*, 1893–94

▼ 6. *Self-Portrait*, 1903

▼ 5. *Self-Portrait (near Golgotha)*, 1896

See also

Learn more about painting people on pages 38–39, and find another Gauguin painting on page 76.

1. Gauguin painted more than 40 self-portraits. This early one shows Gauguin as a young man.

2. Here, Gauguin makes himself look like the hero in the French novel *Les Misérables*. He's saying that artists are heroes, too!

3. Gauguin loved bold colors. Can you see the halo and snake? They might be symbols of good (halo) and evil (snake).

4. At this stage, Gauguin felt successful as an artist. You can see he's included an artist's palette in the painting.

5. This picture's colors are gloomy, and Gauguin looks sad here. The title mentions Golgotha, where Christ died.

6. This is probably Gauguin's last self-portrait. It was painted the year he died, at age 54.

49

Photography

Photos can capture what a person or scene looks like, tell a story, or just create an amazing pattern!

Photographs are made by using light. Early cameras used plastic film to create pictures. Today's digital cameras, tablets, and phones use lots of electrical signals instead.

See also
Find out about a much earlier kind of camera on page 33.

You can take photos of yourself and your friends with a smartphone.

Then and now

People often looked stiff in early photos, as they had to stay still for ages while the picture was being taken. Today, it's easy to snap a quick color selfie on a smartphone camera.

Photo of a young girl, from about 1850.

In the moment

Photos are great for quickly capturing what you happen to see in front of you. French photographer Henri Cartier-Bresson was brilliant at this. This sweet and comic picture shot in Naples, Italy, shows children sleeping at funny angles on deckchairs.

See how the stripy tops and stripy deckchairs make a pattern across the picture.

▲ *Untitled*, Henri Cartier-Bresson, c.1960

▼ *Untitled*, Martin Parr, 2017

Landscape

A landscape photograph shows an outside scene, such as this picture of a beach in St. Ives in Cornwall, England, taken by British photographer Martin Parr. The tiny people surfing with their colorful surfboards play an important part in the picture. They turn the scene into a multicolored pattern.

Portrait

Just as in painting, a photo of someone is called a portrait. This photograph of a herdsman in Rajasthan, India, is by US photographer Steve McCurry.

SPOT IT!

Where else in the book have you seen a red turban like this one?

We can see that the man is a herdsman because of the animals following behind him.

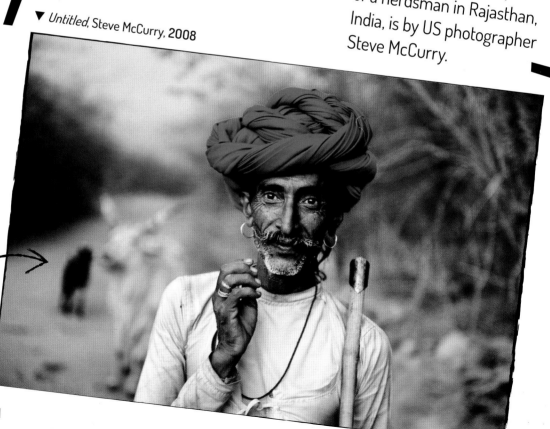

▼ *Untitled*, Steve McCurry, 2008

Painting a moment

When might a painting be like a photograph? When it captures a moment in time.

By the 1890s, a group of French artists called the Impressionists had become very important. In their scenes, they wanted to capture the changes in light, color, and weather that happen outdoors.

Monet took his paints, canvases, and easel outside to paint.

"I am following Nature without being able to grasp her."
Claude Monet

SPOT IT!

Are the shadows long or short in the main picture? What do you think this tells us about the time of day?

Out in the open

French painter Claude Monet is often seen as the leader of the Impressionists. He liked painting pictures of the same subject, such as haystacks, so that he could show the changing light effects at different times of the day and year.

▲ *Haystacks, End of the Summer,* Claude Monet, 1891

See also

Find out more about landscapes on pages 40–41 and light and shadow on pages 36–37.

The long shadows and rich, orange-gold light tell us that it is the end of the day.

Sun and snow

Here you can see that Monet has painted a rich, golden sunset. Below he shows the dazzling effects of sunlight and white snow. Monet often painted outside so he could paint what he saw right away. This is called *plein-air* painting, which means "open air."

Monet painted quickly with lots of short brushstrokes when outside to capture the effect before it was gone.

▲ *Haystacks (Effect of Snow and Sun)*, Claude Monet, 1891

▼ *Combing the Hair ("La Coiffure")*, Edgar Degas, **c.1896**

Scumbling

Scumbling means painting a thin layer of one color loosely over another. Here French artist Degas scumbled whitish paint over the hairdresser's sleeve, which makes the sleeve seem more real.

Whitish paint adds highlights to the sleeve.

Brushstrokes

Artists can choose a certain kind of brushstroke to give them the effect they want. They might paint with strokes of thick paint to show feelings. Or they might use lines or dots of different colors to create texture.

Delicate strokes are used for the ships' masts.

Fine strokes

British artist Turner has added details like the ships' masts with fine and delicate strokes. However, his stormy-looking sky is created with a thin layer of color called a wash.

▲ *Coast Near Brighton*, J.M.W. Turner, **1828**

▼ Mornington Crescent, Summer Morning II, Frank Auerbach, 2004

Thick layers

German–British artist Auerbach is known for using a technique called impasto, where you pile paint on very thickly. You can use a palette knife for this as well as a brush. The paint is so thick that the strokes are easy to see and stand out from the canvas.

Thick paint adds texture.

Which of these four paintings is your favorite?

See also
Discover more about working with paint on pages 24–25.

Dots are added to show a pattern.

Stippling

Stippling means using lots of dotty marks. French artist Matisse uses colorful dots on these carpets to tell us that they are patterned, and to add texture.

▲ Still Life with a Red Carpet, Henri Matisse, 1906

Yellow

How do you feel when you look at the color yellow?

Yellow is a sunny color, but it's also a useful one. Because of its brightness, it is often used in warning signs. Yellow was one of the first colors used in painting.

Ocher pebble

Making yellow

In early times, yellow paint was made from a mineral called ocher. Another yellow paint was made from saffron and was used on paper. Saffron comes from crocus plants and is also a food spice.

Ocher pebble ground down to make a yellow powder

The tips of the strands are bright yellow.

Saffron strands

Forceps fish

Color of nature

Yellow is all around you in nature. It is the color of sunshine. Many butterflies, fish, and flowers come in different shades of yellow.

Cleopatra butterfly

See also

For more about the use of ocher, take a look at page 10.

Sunflowers

This painting by Dutch artist Vincent van Gogh is painted mostly with different shades of yellow. The picture uses thick brushstrokes with lots of paint. The brighter yellow flowers are blooming and the darker ones are dying.

SPOT IT!
Can you see the artist's name on the painting?

""Sunshine ... pale lemon, gold. How lovely yellow is!"
Vincent van Gogh

Scientists say that yellow is a great color for grabbing your attention!

▼ *Entrance of the Port of Honfleur*, Georges Seurat, **1886**

SPOT IT!
Can you see how dots of different colors are used to show reflections in the water?

Lots of dots

Some artists use lots and lots of dots to make their pictures.

The colors look fairly normal in the painting above. But close up, you see that they are made up of thousands of separate, colored dots. This technique is called Pointillism, and it was very popular in the late 1800s. Can you see how this method has made the colors bright and rich?

See also
You'll find more dots on pages 86–87.

Tricking the eye

Instead of mixing colors on a palette, your eye mixes dots of color together as you look at the picture from farther away. This scientific process is called optical mixing. It is a trick your brain plays on you.

> **"Some say they see poetry in my paintings; I see only science."**
>
> Georges Seurat

UP CLOSE! The dots work like pixels on a computer screen.

SPOT IT!

How is Trang's picture different from Seurat's?

Phan Thu Trang

This painting is by Phan Thu Trang, who comes from Hanoi in Vietnam. Like Seurat, she loves light and color. She uses dots, and also larger dabs of color.

Can you see how light falling on water makes it look dotty?

Children

For many centuries, children in art didn't seem like children. They were made to look serious and were just like adults.

In fact, very few pictures showed children at all. Then, in the 1700s, people started to be interested in what children thought and did. By the end of the 1800s, they were a favorite subject in paintings. Artists showed them doing the normal things children love to do, such as playing, having fun, and reading.

Children dressed exactly like adults in the 1700s.

SPOT IT!
Can you see a writing pen in this picture (left)?

Spinning a top

French artist Jean-Baptiste-Siméon Chardin was one of the first artists to show children being themselves. This little boy should be doing his homework, but he's spinning a top instead!

▲ *Child with a Spinning Top*, Jean-Siméon Chardin, c.1738

▲ *Little Girl in a Blue Armchair*, Mary Cassatt, 1878

The brushstrokes are very loose and lively.

Taking it easy

American painter Mary Cassatt has used energetic brushstrokes in this painting. But having lots of calming blue color also makes the picture restful. This mix is like the little girl—she was playing but now she's flopped into the chair. Do you think she looks tired, relaxed, or bored?

SPOT IT!
The picture (left) seems more relaxing because her little dog is resting, too!

See also

Find more pictures of children on pages 15, 25, 31, 38, 45, 50, 64, 65, 81, and 86–87.

Reading

The girl here looks lost in her own little world of reading. The picture was painted on a wall by French street artist Jef Aérosol. The pretty butterflies fluttering around her make you think that she is reading a happy story!

▲ *Read Dream*, Jef Aérosol, 2014

Bluebird

Shades of blue

Blues range from pale and delicate blue flowers to the darkest blue-black of the night sky. The blue ground beetle shines with a metallic blue, while bluebirds can have many different shades of blue in their feathers.

Blue ground beetle

Himalayan blue poppy

Blue

Blue is the color of coolness, calm, the sky, water, and sadness.

Blue is clear, clean, refreshing, and holy. In the Middle Ages (1000s–1400s) and afterwards, many artists loved ultramarine blue, and often used it in religious paintings.

Lapis lazuli

Cobalt blue powder

A powder made with cobalt is used for paint.

Azurite

Making blue

Lapis lazuli means "blue stone." It was used to make an artists' blue called ultramarine. This beautiful shade of blue was precious because lapis is rare. The mineral azurite makes a similar blue and it was cheaper.

Blue is one of the three primary paint colors. Do you know what the other two are?

Ultramarine blue

Can you see the soft folds in this bright ultramarine cloak? Like many artists of the time, Italian painter Sassoferrato gave Jesus' mother Mary a cloak painted in this precious blue, to show that she was a special and holy person.

See also

Discover more about primary colors on pages 8–9 and how blue is used to show distance on pages 20–21.

▲ *The Virgin in Prayer*, Sassoferrato, 1640–50

Showing feelings

▲ *Mystical Head: Woman's Head on a Blue Background*, Alexei von Jawlensky, c.1917

Showing how we feel can be more important than showing things.

Calm

Artist Alexei von Jawlensky was Russian, but spent most of his life in Germany. There, he became part of a big art movement called German Expressionism. The cool blue background of the painting gives it a calm feeling.

SPOT IT!
See how this woman has yellow lips!

What kind of picture might you make if you felt calm …

Any artists who show, or express, strong feelings in their art are often called "expressionist." There was also an art movement called Expressionism in the early 1900s. These artists often used bold, unusual colors and strong brushstrokes to express feelings.

See also

Learn about Abstract Expressionism on page 79.

"You should not paint the chair, but only what someone has felt about it." Edvard Munch

Anxious

Norwegian artist Edvard Munch was an early Expressionist. He had a lot of unhappiness in his life. The main person in the painting looks anxious and is letting out a big scream. The picture is filled with wild, swirly lines, and the sunset sky looks like it is on fire.

SPOT IT!

Can you see two people walking together on the bridge?

... How about if you felt worried?

▶ *The Scream*, Edvard Munch, 1893

The person is made of swirly lines like the surrounding landscape.

What other expressions on your face could you have and how might you show them?

Colorful shapes

The space in this painting by Braque looks squashed and the buildings are made from simple geometrical (regular) shapes. It is said that Cubism got its name when someone described Braque's art as being like strange cubes.

See also
You'll find different ways of looking at space and distance on pages 20–21.

▲ *The Viaduct at L'Estaque*, Georges Braque, 1908

▼ *Bibémus Quarry*, Paul Cézanne, c.1895

New angles

In the early 1900s, artists looked at art from a different angle ...

Artists Pablo Picasso and Georges Braque invented an amazing new style called Cubism. This style used lots of broken-up, geometric (regular) shapes, together with areas or blocks of color. In their paintings, they included views from different angles at the same time, to make you feel you were seeing in 3-D.

Early Cubism

Even as early as the 1800s, French artist Paul Cézanne painted using simpler shapes. This inspired the Cubist artists. In this picture, some things look flat and some don't. Do you think it is like Braque's picture?

> **"I paint objects as I think them, not as I see them."** *Pablo Picasso*

Dora Maar with Cat, Pablo Picasso, 1941

SPOT IT!

Can you see the cat in the painting? Does it look like a real one?

Fang mask, Gabon, Africa, late 1800s–early 1900s

A different kind of real

Spanish artist Pablo Picasso continued to paint Cubist-like pictures, such as this one, into the 1940s. You can see that this is a woman, even though her face is a funny color and is shown from different angles. Dora Maar had beautiful hands in real life, but they are more like sharp claws here.

African mask

The shapes, forms, and styles of African masks and sculptures inspired artists such as Picasso to look at art in a new way.

67

Some green paints used in the past were dangerous. They contained the poison arsenic!

▲ *Exotic Landscape*, Henri Rousseau, 1910

More than one green

We think that French artist Henri Rousseau used more than 20 shades of green in some of his landscapes. Here, he adds oranges. Can you see how orange helps bring out the shades of green?

SPOT IT!
Can you see a monkey catching oranges?

Making green

Verdigris was a popular green-blue paint pigment made from copper and vinegar. A mineral called malachite was also used to make green.

Green copper sheet

Putting copper into vinegar makes a green layer form on the surface.

Malachite

Green

This is the color of nature and life.

The word "green" comes from the verb "to grow" and is linked with nature. It is a restful color that is also a symbol of new life, freshness, and growth. It may be that there are more shades of green than any other color.

See also

Learn more about how contrasting colors work on pages 8–9.

Mint green

Apple green

Color of nature

A lot of the words we use to describe shades of green are linked to nature. For instance, mint green and apple green are used to describe fresh, bright shades of green. Can you think of another fruit that is also a shade of green?

▼ *The Sheaf*, Henri Matisse, 1953

Paper cutting

Creating colorful cutout paper shapes is popular around the world.

Many celebrations and festivals feature paper shapes, such as confetti at weddings and paper-cut pictures at the Chinese Spring Festival. Paper shapes can be made into collages by arranging them into a picture and pasting onto a flat surface.

SPOT IT!
Can you spot any two shapes that are exactly the same?

Henri Matisse used several different sizes of scissors for his cutouts.

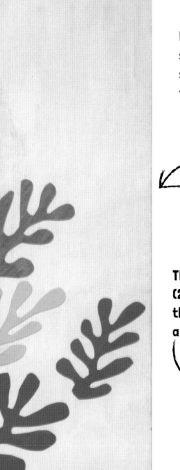

The leafy shapes show joy in nature.

The cutout is 9½ ft (2.9 m) high—more than twice the size of a nine-year-old child!

HM 53

Bold and simple

The Sheaf collage is one of the last works of French artist Henri Matisse. The paper shapes are painted with a thick watercolor paint called gouache.

▼ *Times Square*, Béatrice Coron, 2014

Béatrice Coron

Like Matisse, Béatrice Coron is French. This artwork shows New York City, where she moved to in the 1980s. It is cut out of fabric, but the artist also cuts paper. Coron likes telling stories. Her silhouettes are cut from a single sheet, bringing a story together and adding some fairytale magic.

"There are always flowers for those who want to see them."
Henri Matisse

See also
You can learn more about the use of shapes in art on pages 6–7, 66–67, and 78–79.

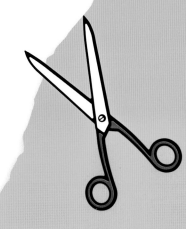

Dreams and imaginings

Have you noticed how your dreams might be odd but seem real when you are having them?

In the 1920s and 1930s, one group of artists made works that were strange or dreamlike. They were called the Surrealists. The word Surrealism comes from the French for "super reality." Some paintings had parts that looked real, and parts that looked impossible.

See also
Look at some other fantastical art on pages 80–81 and 86–87.

▶ The Son of Man, René Magritte, 1964

The unexpected

Belgian painter René Magritte created this ordinary-looking, nicely dressed character. But why is an apple hiding his face? Surrealists liked to mix ordinary and unlikely things together to surprise people.

"The mind loves the unknown."
René Magritte

Funny fantasy

Surrealists were interested in the thoughts and dreams locked away in our brains. Spanish artist Salvador Dalí created these fun elephants with skinny rather than chunky legs!

SPOT IT!

Are the elephants carrying those heavy stone sculptures?

The sky makes us think of other dreamlike worlds.

▼ Project for "As You Like It," Salvador Dalí, **1948**

▼ *Figure, Dog, Birds*, Joan Miró, **1946**

Painting by instinct

Spanish artist Joan Miró liked to paint freely. He created many doodly pictures like this one. Can you pick out a person, a dog, and some birds? Some people think Miró's paintings look like cave art.

Symbols in art

Feelings and ideas can be hard to show in art, so artists often use real things, such as flowers or animals, instead. Symbols can mean more than one thing. For example, a sun might be a symbol of light or heat.

See also
Uncover other mysterious symbols on pages 36–37.

▼ *The Arnolfini Portrait*, Jan van Eyck, **1434**

▼ *King Cophetua and the Beggar Maid*, Edward Burne-Jones, **1884**

Married couple

Artist Jan van Eyck came from modern-day Belgium. The artist includes oranges in this picture of a couple at home in Bruges, in Belgium, to symbolize that they were wealthy. Oranges were rare and expensive in Belgium at this time.

Wooing a maid

This painting tells the story of a king falling in love with a poor girl. The crown on the king's lap shows that the king thinks love and beauty are more important than power and riches.

Can you find these symbols in the paintings?

Bouquet

Flowers, symbolizing love, appear in two of these paintings!

Crown

In the painting, the crown symbolizes royalty and wealth.

Oranges

In the painting, oranges are a symbol of wealth.

Dog

Dogs are often a symbol of loyalty.

▼ *The Birthday*, Marc Chagall, 1915

Happy together

This painting shows Russian-French artist Marc Chagall and his wife Bella. They are so in love they are floating on air! The flowers make you think of love. Chagall liked symbols. Some of his symbols came from traditional Russian folk art.

"I had only to open my window, and blue sky, love and flowers entered with her."

Marc Chagall

P Gauguin - 92

SPOT IT!

Can you see part of a mango tree anywhere in the picture?

New colors

Between 1891 and 1893, French artist Paul Gauguin went to the island of Tahiti, in the Pacific Ocean. He painted this Tahitian woman there. Gauguin used Tahiti's bold colors in his work. They looked very modern for the 1800s. The purple dress stands out strongly against the yellow background.

Royal colors

For centuries, only rich people wore purple, as the dye came from snails and was hard to make. In 1856, the first synthetic purple dye was made, so more people could wear purple.

Empress Eugénie

This French empress led a fashion craze for purple!

Purple

Purple is a mix of cool blue and warm and powerful red!

Purple is the color of luxury and power, worn by Roman emperors, kings and queens, and popes. It can also mean creativity, wisdom, and mystery.

Making purple

From early times, artists usually made purple by mixing blue and red. In the 1860s, a purple paint, called manganese violet, was invented. Now purple came straight from a tube!

Sea urchin

Lavender

Amethyst

Purple in nature

Purple can be found all around us in nature, from lavender flowers and prickly sea urchins to sparkly amethyst stones.

See also

Find out more about how colors work together on pages 8–9 and pages 68–69.

Shapes and colors

▼ *Composition with Large Red Plane, Yellow, Black, Grey and Blue*, Piet Mondrian, **1921**

Many artists believe that shapes, colors, and lines used on their own make good pictures.

This is called abstract art. Abstract artists think that what they paint doesn't have to look like something we could easily recognize—such as a person, a thing, or a scene.

Squared up

Dutch artist Piet Mondrian made pictures from rectangles and squares. Many of his paintings used the three primary colors of red, yellow, and blue.

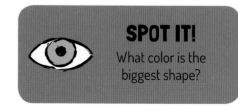

SPOT IT!
What color is the biggest shape?

▼ *Convergence*, Jackson Pollock, 1952

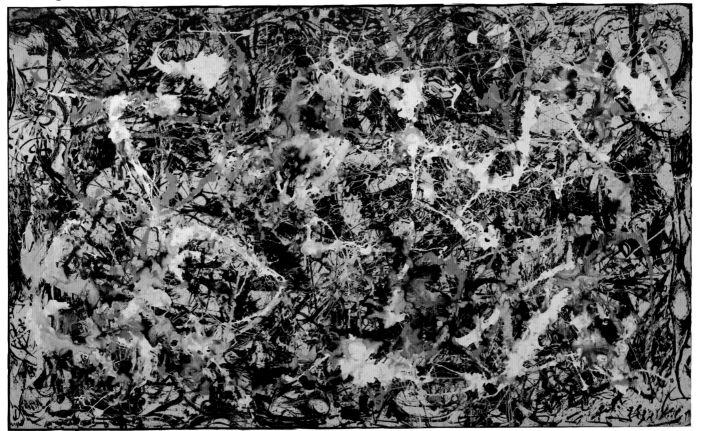

Splattered paint

American artist Jackson Pollock made colorful and lively paintings. He was part of a group called the Abstract Expressionists. A puzzle company made a jigsaw puzzle based on this picture. It was said to be the world's hardest puzzle!

The picture is 155 x 93½ in (394 x 237 cm)—about twice the height of a seven-year-old child.

UP CLOSE! Pollock poured, dribbled, and splashed paint across the canvas to get this effect.

See also

You can learn more about how shapes and colors can be used on pages 6–7 and 8–9.

Fun art

In the 1960s, Pop Art got its name from having fun with popular objects in modern life.

By the 1960s, the world was changing fast. People wanted modern things that made life easier. They also wanted to have more fun. Pop artists showed this new life. Some made bold, colorful art that looked like comics. They painted things that people saw and bought everyday, including food!

Soup cans

American artist Andy Warhol repeated images of the same thing, like these screenprints of soup cans, to make his work seem more like advertisements or products in a shop than "art." Warhol wanted people to see that popular things were art, too.

See also
Discover another artist who liked to paint lots of pictures of the same thing on pages 52–53.

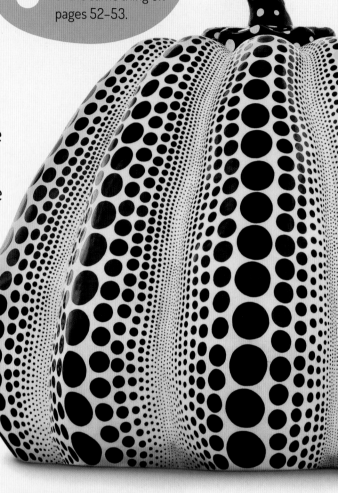

▲ *Campbell's Soup Cans*, Andy Warhol, 1965

In the 1960s, acrylic paint was very popular with Pop artists. It dried faster than oils, and was ideal for making big areas of bold, flat color.

Yellow pumpkin

Japanese artist Yayoi Kusama loves to make dotty art! This sculpture of a yellow pumpkin with black dots stands on Naoshima island in Japan.

The pumpkin is about 7 ft (2.2 m) high—that's taller than an adult!

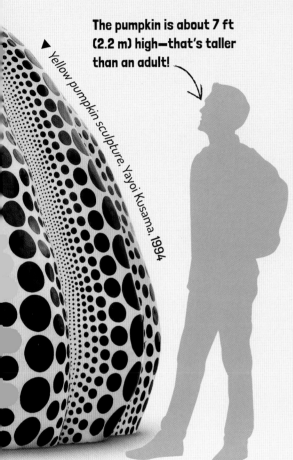

▲ *Yellow pumpkin sculpture, Yayoi Kusama, 1994*

Plates of pie

American artist Wayne Thiebaud has made this colorful picture from repeats of the same thing, like Warhol's cans. He liked showing popular US foods by using simple geometrical (regular) shapes.

"I want to be plastic." Andy Warhol

Acrylic hot dog

British Pop artist Peter Blake loved American culture—such as hot dogs! This boy looks like he has just popped up in front of a camera. Blake painted this in acrylic paint. It helped him make the sky very blue and flat, and to give a sharp edge to the green hill.

▲ *Boy Eating a Hot Dog*, Peter Blake, 1960–65

This man is an important knight, so he wears black. Italian artist Moroni shows light and shade in the clothes, even though they are dark. The white cuffs and collar make a bright contrast.

Black and white are bold opposites. In art, they often stand for darkness and light. Black can mean wealth and importance. Its links with darkness also make it ideal for showing bad things. White makes us think of childhood, purity, and goodness.

Making black

Charcoal is made by burning wood. It is one of the oldest blacks, and is found in cave paintings. You can draw with it or use it in paint.

Charcoal

Crow

Witch's hat

What does black mean?

In art, black can be used for night, for sad or bad things, and for witches, magic, and mystery. Witches wear black and crows mean bad luck in some countries, but good luck in others!

▲ *The Knight in Black*, Giovanni Battista Moroni, 1567

white

Chalk

Oyster shell

Making white

Chalk, a soft rock, has been used for white ever since cave art. It is good for drawing and for adding to some paints. Japanese artists use a white pigment made from crushed oyster shells.

See also
Take a look at the striking black-and-white picture on page 12.

Milk

Lily

What does white mean?

What kinds of white things can you think of? Milk, lilies, snow, and clouds are just some things that you might think of. White often makes us think of clean, fresh things that are unspoiled and fragile.

White maiden

Here, American artist Whistler uses lots of different whites to add interest. See how he uses white for adding bright areas and for telling us that this is a young, innocent girl at the start of her adult life.

▲ *Symphony in White, No. 1: The White Girl*, James McNeill Whistler, **1862**

▼ *Opus III*, Victor Vasarely, 1970-74

Tricking the eye

Look out—these paintings might make your eyes go funny!

Around the 1960s, some artists made pictures based on optical illusions that trick our eyes. They showed how the eye and brain work together to understand color, shape, space, and movement. This art was called Op Art.

See also

You'll find another picture by Victor Vasarely on page 12 and other dotty pictures on pages 58–59 and 86–87.

Disappearing squares

Op artists liked to repeat simple patterns, geometric shapes, and strong colors. Hungarian-French artist Victor Vasarely often used shapes that got smaller and smaller to make flat surfaces look like they were being sucked down into a central point.

▼ Hermann grid illusion, 1870

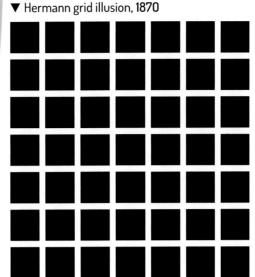

Grid illusion

This optical illusion is called a "Hermann grid." Op artists used effects like this in their work. Can you see ghostly grey dots where the squares meet? When you stare hard at one crossing point, no dot appears at all.

Studying painters like Georges Seurat, who also painted with dots, helped to give Bridget Riley ideas about Op effects.

SPOT IT!

Can you see how the circles change to flatter ovals as you go deeper into the picture?

Moving dots

This painting by British artist Bridget Riley shows rows of circles followed by rows of oval shapes. Bands of pale and dark shapes cross the picture. All this makes the painting seem to move like a wave.

▲ *Hesitate*, Bridget Riley, 1964

Art today

▼ *Obliteration Room* (start), Yayoi Kusama, **2000s**

▼ *Obliteration Room* (middle)

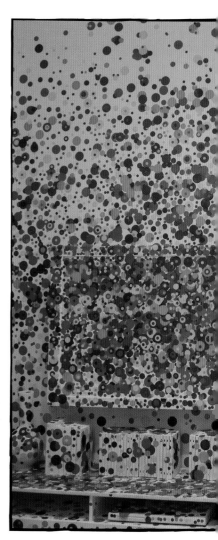

Artists have always liked to try new things.

For lots of artists, art is all about trying different or unusual things to show us how they are feeling. Art can be made from just about any material you want. Modern artists might draw on a smartphone screen, make a film or a light show, record sounds, wrap a building, or paint with chocolate sauce! What ideas can you think of?

Installation art

Installation art is made from a mix of materials and can take up a lot of space. It often creates its own little world. This work by British artist Lubaina Himid has 100 life-size figures, each one cut out and painted.

Performance art

Performance art is made by people's actions. Japanese artist Yayoi Kusama created this *Obliteration Room* project. The room was totally white and then she asked people to cover the white surfaces with round, colored stickers.

◀ *Obliteration Room* (end), Yayoi Kusama, **2000s**

SPOT IT!
What musical instrument can you see in the room?

◀ *Naming the Money*, Lubaina Himid, **2000s**

Digital art

British artist Andrew Macara makes oil paintings full of color and light effects. Here, he does the same thing—but he is using a painting app to create a digital picture on a tablet screen!

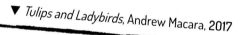

▼ *Tulips and Ladybirds*, Andrew Macara, **2017**

See also

See more fun art on pages 80–81 and other dotted pictures on pages 58–59.

Timeline

These pages show important artists, ideas, and art movements throughout history. Many appear in the book, and you'll see some new ones here, too! All the terms are explained in the glossary in the back.

30,000 BCE

5000 BCE

1000 BCE

600 CE

1400

Renaissance

This was a special time when artists like Italian artist Michelangel[o] mixed old ideas from the past with exciting new ones[.]

▲ *Pietà*, Michelangelo, 1497–1500

Leonardo da Vinci

This great Italian Renaissance artist was also a scientist and even invented flying machines!

Born 1452; died 1519

Cave painting
Thousands of years ago people painted great art on rocks and inside caves.

▲ Cave painting, Lascaux, France, c.15,000 BCE

Early China
In China, artists were now expert at making prints as well as paintings on silk like this one.

◀ Detail from *The Spinning Wheel*, Wang Juzheng, mid-1000s

Islamic art
Islamic art often used delicate patterns from flowers and plants, like this beautiful jug from Turkey.

▲ Turkish "Iznik" style jug, 1500s

▼ Detail of a wall painting of the god Atum, Tomb of Nefertari, Egypt, c.1200s BCE

Ancient Egypt
The Ancient Egyptians made paintings on the walls of royal people's tombs.

▼ Statuette of Zeus, 200s BCE

Ancient Greece
Artists in ancient Greece made beautiful sculptures.

▼ Mosaic, Basilica (church) of Sant'Apollinare Nuovo, Ravenna, Italy, 500s

Early Rome
Italy has played a huge part in art from earliest times. The Italians made some marvelous mosaics!

▼ *The Tiger Hunt*, Peter Paul Rubens, c.1616

German artist Friedrich was part of a "Romantic" movement that showed how people felt about nature.

Caspar David Friedrich

Born 1774; died 1840

▼ *La Fileuse* (The Spinning Girl), J.-F. Millet, 1868–69

Baroque
In the 1600s, Baroque artists, such as Flemish (Belgian) painter Rubens, made ornate, dramatic art.

▼ *The Fighting Temeraire*, J.M.W. Turner, 1839

Realism
In the mid-1800s, art started to show the lives of ordinary people in a very real way. This was called Realism.

1850

1600

Landscape
Painting landscapes was now in fashion. British artist Turner was skilled at showing real seas and skies.

Things were changing in art as the world got more modern ... turn the page to find out how ...

Rembrandt

Born 1606; died 1669

Art was getting more realistic now. Dutch artist Rembrandt was a genius at portraits. He painted many of himself.

1700

1800

Rachel Ruysch

Dutch painter Rachel Ruysch's still lifes of fruit and flowers were so detailed, they looked like the real thing!

Born 1664; died 1750

Constable was another great British landscape artist. He made skies of sparkly sunlight and dramatic clouds!

John Constable

Born 1776; died 1837

▼ *The Lacemaker*, Johannes Vermeer, c.1669–70

At home
Art showing everyday life at home started to become popular in the 1600s. This painting is by Dutch artist Vermeer.

Japanese woodblock
Japanese artist Hokusai used wooden blocks to make his prints. European artists working at the end of the 1800s loved his works.

▼ *The Great Wave*, Hokusai, c.1830–31

French landscape art started moving toward Impressionism.

Impressionism
French Impressionist artists were painting exciting new pictures outside, on the spot.

► *Monet in his Studio Boat,* Édouard Manet, 1874

Pablo Picasso
Born 1881; died 1973

Spanish artist Picasso was still making Cubist-like pictures in the 1940s, but made other amazing modern art, too.

1870

1880

Vincent van Gogh

Dutch painter van Gogh's emotional, colorful paintings were a type of early Expressionism.

Born 1853; died 1890

Georges Seurat

French artist Seurat made pictures using lots and lots of dots.

Born 1859; died 1891

1890

Frida Kahlo

Born 1907; died 1954

Mexican artist Kahlo mixed together Expressionism and Surrealism.

Edvard Munch

Born 1863; died 1944

Like van Gogh, Norwegian artist Munch painted his feelings in a colorful way.

1900

The first truly abstract pictures were made just after 1900.

▼ *Still Life: Le Jour,* Georges Braque, 1929

Cubism
Cubism was invented by Braque and Picasso. It made objects look flattened and broken up.

1910

1920

▼ *Composition VII,* Wassily Kandinsky, 1913

1930

1940

Expressionism
In the early 1900s, Expressionist art was bold, colorful, and emotional. Russian artist Kandinksy made this abstract picture.

Surrealism
Spaniard Dalí and other Surrealists put things together in a crazy way.

▲ *Lobster Telephone,* Salvador Dalí, 1936

◀ *Icarus*, plate VIII from *Jazz*, Henri Matisse, 1947

Barbara Hepworth

Born 1903; died 1975

British artist Hepworth made abstract curvy and geometric sculptures from the 1930s to the 1960s.

▼ *In the Car*, Roy Lichtenstein, 1963

Pop Art
Pop artists such as American artist Lichtenstein made fun art that looked like comics or advertisements.

Paper cutting
French artist Matisse's simple, colorful paper cutouts influenced 1960s art.

Bridget Riley

Born 1931

In the 1960s, Op Art was very popular. British painter Riley made amazing art from optical illusions.

1950

1960

1970

Jackson Pollock

Born 1912; died 1956

American artist Pollock was an Abstract Expressionist. In the 1940s and '50s he shocked people with his abstract "drip" art.

Artists loved using acrylic paint in the 1960s.

1980

In the 1970s, art became more experimental—art could do anything and everything!

Jean-Michel Basquiat

Born 1960; died 1988

American artist Basquiat made people take graffiti and street art more seriously.

1990

2000

2010

Abstract
Around 1950, American artist Mark Rothko started making famous abstract paintings featuring large areas of color.

By the 2000s, people were buying experimental art for huge amounts of money!

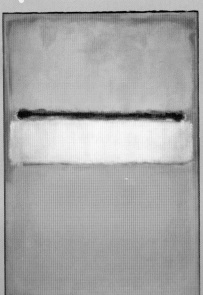

◀ *White Center (Yellow, Pink and Lavender on Rose)*, Mark Rothko, 1950

Art today
Film, performance art, or sculpture like Japanese artist Kusama's flowers. Anything is possible today. What new art ideas can you think of?

▲ *Flowers That Bloom Tomorrow*, Yayoi Kusama, 2010

Glossary

Here are some important words that are used when talking about art.

abstract art
Art that doesn't look like the real world and is made of lines, shapes, or colors

Abstract Expressionism
Art movement in the US. The artworks are abstract and bold. They express the artists' feelings very strongly and are often really big

acrylic paint
Modern paint that dries quickly and can make bright, bold colors

artwork
Any kind of piece of art, like a painting, drawing, sculpture, or installation

Baroque
Art that is dramatic, bold, and often very ornate

camera obscura
Simple, early camera that some artists used to plan their work

canvas
Type of cloth on which many oil paintings are painted

cave painting
Painting on the rock wall of a cave

color wheel
Way of showing paint colors in the shape of a wheel to see how they work together

complementary colors
Colors that contrast with each other. They are opposite each other on the color wheel

composition
How things, such as people or animals, trees, mountains, skies, shapes, and colors, are arranged in a piece of art

Cubism
Art that looks broken up and flat, and is trying to show things from lots of different angles

culture
The art, science, beliefs, and everyday lives of a particular group of people

design
Arranged pattern. Also a plan for how something might look when it is finished

detail
Just one part of a picture or work, and not the whole thing

digital art
Art made by using computers, tablets, or smartphones

dye
Substance you use to turn something a different color

egg tempera
Fast-drying paint made by mixing eggs and pigment

exhibition
When artists make a display of their work so that people can come and see it

Expressionism
Art that expresses strong feelings or ideas. It often uses bold, unusual colors, and might not look very realistic

fresco
Type of wall painting made by painting onto wet plaster

geometric
Basic shapes such as circles, squares, rectangles, cubes, and ovals

glaze
Thin, see-through layer of paint

gold leaf
Thin sheets of real gold

graffiti art
Words or pictures scribbled or painted outside on buildings and walls, often with spray paint, for anyone to see

halo
Shiny circle seen around the heads of important people in Christian paintings

horizon
Where the sea or land meets the sky

impasto
Bold brushstrokes with thick paint

Impressionism
French art movement that captured weather effects as they changed and used looser brushstrokes than many earlier artists

installation
Big, mixed-media works that often fill a space, such as a room full of painted, cutout figures that you can walk in between

Islamic art
Art connected to the religion of Islam and Islamic areas, such as Persia (now Iran) and Turkey. Islamic art often has patterns based on plants and geometric shapes

landscape
Picture that shows somewhere outside in nature, such as mountains or fields

lapis lazuli
Precious rock used to make a beautiful, bright-blue paint called ultramarine

lifelike
When something looks just like it does in real life

life-size
The same size as in real life

mineral
Rocks from the ground used to make pigments

mixed media
When different materials are used in the same artwork, such as watercolor paint alongside pencil and crayon

movement
Group of artists who all have the same kind of artistic ideas. Impressionism, Cubism, and Expressionism are all art movements

mural
Painting on a wall that often covers a whole wall

ocher
Important pigment for making paints with earthy colors, such as dark yellow

oil paint
Paint made by mixing pigment and oil. It dries slowly, so it's easy to make changes and fix mistakes

opaque
Layer of paint that you can't see through

Op Art
Style of art that uses optical illusions to make your eyes see weird things in pictures

optical illusion
Optical means to do with eyes. Optical illusions are pictures that trick your eyes into seeing something that isn't really there, such as moving lines

palette
Type of board or tray you use so that you have paints ready as you paint. You can also mix your paints on it

pattern
If you repeated a picture of the same flower over and over in a nicely arranged way in a painting, that would be a pattern. Wallpaper is often patterned

perspective
Set of lines invented in the Renaissance period that helped artists to show space and distance in a realistic way

pigment
This gives paint its color. It is often made of ground-up minerals

plaster
Fast-drying paste that often covers walls

Pointillism
Art that's made of separate colored dots

Pop Art
Art that was all about popular, modern everyday life

portrait
Picture where the main subject is a person. Some portraits have more than one person in them

pose
The position of a person in an artwork, such as standing

primary colors
The three main paint colors—red, yellow, and blue. You can make all other colors by mixing these colors in different ways

print
Picture made in a way that means you can repeat it over and over again

Renaissance
Period in the 1400s and 1500s when artists had lots of new ideas, such as perspective

Romantic
Word often used in a special way in art. Artists of the Romantic art movement were interested in people's personal thoughts and feelings as well as showing lovely landscapes

scene
What you see in front of you and choose to make a picture of, such as someone sitting reading or a beach

sculpture
Solid, 3-D (three-dimensional) artwork made from material like stone or wood

self-portrait
Piece of art made by an artist that shows the artist themselves

sketch
A drawing done quickly. You might make a pencil sketch to prepare for making a painting

still life
Picture that's a careful arrangement of objects, such as fruit or flowers

street art
Art that people make out in the street, usually on walls, such as graffiti art

style
A certain way of showing things in a painting. The Expressionists used a style with unusual colors and bold brushstrokes

subject
What a work of art is about, such as a group of friends or a vase of flowers

Surrealism
Art that puts odd things together in a crazy or dreamlike way

symbol
Something that stands for something else. A picture of a crown, for example, often means a king or queen

Symbolism
Art movement that uses a lot of symbols

transparent
A layer of paint you can see through

trompe l'oeil
Painting that is so realistic you think what's painted is really there in front of you

vanishing point
Point in the center and in the distance of a picture using perspective lines

watercolor
Paint made by mixing pigment and water, often used for light, see-through effects

wet-on-wet
When artists paint into paint that is already wet

woodblock print
Type of print made by carving a picture into a block of wood

Index

Acknowledgments

The publisher would like to thank the following people for their assistance in the preparation of this book: Jane Findlay from the Dulwich Picture Gallery (consultancy); Phil Hunt (editorial help); Helen Peters (index); Polly Goodman (proofreading); Xiao Lin (additional illustrations)

The publisher would like to thank the following for their kind permission to reproduce their photographs: (Key: a-above; b-below/bottom; c-center; f-far; l-left; r-right; t-top)

6-7 Bridgeman Images: Mondadori Portfolio / Walter Mori / © Successió Miró / ADAGP, Paris and DACS London 2018. 9 akg-images. 10-11 Getty Images: DEA Picture Library / De Agostini (t). 10 Dorling Kindersley: Winsor & Newton (fcl). Dreamstime.com: Fokinol (clb/ochre). 11 Getty Images: Robert Harding (br). 12 Bridgeman Images: Private Collection / Phillips, Fine Art Auctioneers, New York / © ADAGP, Paris and DACS, London 2018 (cra); Stadtische Galerie im Lenbachhaus, Munich, Germany / Artothek (tl). 13 Bridgeman Images: National Gallery, London (l); Victoria & Albert Museum, London / Photo © David Pearson (tr). 14 Bridgeman Images: De Agostini Picture Library / S. Vannini (t); Universal History Archive / UIG (b). 15 123RF.com: Rodrigo Mello Nunes / rmnunes (tl). Alamy Stock Photo: Peter Mross / alltravel / © DACS 2018 (c). 16 akg-images: Pictures From History (bl). Dorling Kindersley: The Trustees of the British Museum (tr). 17 Bridgeman Images: National Gallery, London (l). Flinders Lane Gallery: © Christine Michaels / Copyright Agency. Licensed by DACS 2018 (tr). 18 Bridgeman Images: Louvre, Paris (tl, bl); Museo di San Marco, Florence (c). 19 Bridgeman Images: Ashmolean Museum, University of Oxford (tr). 20 Bridgeman Images: National Gallery, London. 21 Bridgeman Images: National Gallery, London. 22 akg-images: Erich Lessing (bl). Dreamstime.com: Ilyach (tl). Getty Images: DeAgostini / A. Dagli Orti (cb/coin). 23 123RF.com: artenex (r/gold background). Bridgeman Images: Neue Galerie, New York / De Agostini Picture Library / E. Lessing. 24 akg-images: (cl, bl); WHA / World History Archive (cr, br). 25 akg-images: (cl, cr, bl, br). 26 Bridgeman Images: Bauhaus Archive, Berlin / © DACS 2018 (bl). Dreamstime.com: Karayuschij (bl). 27 Bridgeman Images: Private Collection / Photo © Christie's Images / © ADAGP, Paris and DACS, London 2018. 28 Bridgeman Images: De Agostini Picture Library / G. Dagli Orti (bl); The Hepworth Wakefield, West Yorkshire / Hepworth © Bowness (r). 29 Alamy Stock Photo: David Herraez / © The Easton Foundation / DACS, London / VAGA, NY 2018 (tr). Bridgeman Images: Omniphoto / UIG (br). 30 akg-images: (tl); The National Gallery, London (tr). 31 akg-images: © Estate of Duane Hanson / DACS, London / VAGA, NY 2018 (tr). Bridgeman Images: Saint Louis Art Museum, Missouri, USA / Funds given by Mr. and Mrs. R. Crosby Kemper Jr. through the Crosby Kemper Foundations, The Arthur and Helen Baer Charitable Foundation, Mr. and Mrs. Van-Lear Black III, Anabeth Calkins and John Weil, Mr. and Mrs. Gary Wolff, the Honorable and Mrs. Thomas / © Gerhard Richter 2018 (0141) (bl). 32 akg-images: Heritage-Images / Art Media (tr). Bridgeman Images: Private Collection (bl). 33 Photo Scala, Florence: Foto Fine Art Images / Heritage Images. 34 Bridgeman Images: Prado, Madrid. 35 Getty Images: Paul Starosta / Corbis (tr/cochineal). 36-37 Alamy Stock Photo: Fototeca Gilardi (cb). 36 akg-images: Fototeca Gilardi. 37 akg-images: Fototeca Gilardi (tr, cr, br). 38 Bridgeman Images: Dulwich Picture Gallery, London (br). 39 Bridgeman Images: Museo Dolores Olmedo Patino, Mexico City, Mexico / De Agostini Picture Library / © Banco de México Diego Rivera Frida Kahlo Museums Trust, Mexico, D.F. / DACS 2018 (t). ©Tate, London 2018: David Hockney I "My Parents" 1977 I Oil on canvas I 72 x 72" I © David Hockney I Collection Tate, U.K. (br). 40 Alamy Stock Photo: National Gallery, London. 41 Bridgeman Images: Hamburger Kunsthalle, Hamburg. 42 akg-images: De Agostini Picture Library (bl, crb/detail). Alamy Stock Photo: Paul Fearn (tl, cra/detail). 43 Bridgeman Images: Museum der Stadt, Ulm, Germany (br, clb/detail); Private Collection (tr, cla/detail). 44 Alamy Stock Photo: Shawn Hempel (fbl). 45 Photo Scala, Florence: Album. 46-47 Photo Scala, Florence: courtesy of the Ministero Beni e Att. Culturali e del Turismo (c). 46 Dreamstime.com: Burtonhill (br); Ppy2010ha (clb/peach). 47 123RF.com: Andrzej Tokarski / ajt (cra/snail). Dorling Kindersley: Thomas Marent (fcra). 48 akg-images: (r). Bridgeman Images: Fogg Art Museum, Harvard Art Museums, USA / Gift of Helen W. Ellsworth in memory of Duncan S. Ellsworth '22, nephew of Archibald A. Hutchinson, benefactor of the Hutchinson Wing, 1996.218 (tl); Van Gogh Museum, Amsterdam (cb). 49 akg-images: (tr); Cameraphoto (tc). Bridgeman Images: Museu de Arte, Sao Paulo, Brazil / De Agostini Picture Library / E. Lessing (cb). 50 123RF.com: Wavebreak Media Ltd (cra). Alamy Stock Photo: age fotostock (cl). Magnum Photos: © Henri Cartier-Bresson (b). 51 Magnum Photos: © Steve McCurry (br); © Martin Parr (tl). 52 Bridgeman Images: Musée d'Orsay, Paris (b). 53 akg-images: (tr). Bridgeman Images: Metropolitan Museum of Art, New York (br). 54 akg-images: (bl, crb/detail); The National Gallery, London (tl, cra/detail). 55 Bridgeman Images: Ben Uri Gallery, The London Jewish Museum of Art / © Frank Auerbach, courtesy Marlborough Fine Art (tr, cla/detail); Archives Henri Matisse: © Succession H. Matisse / DACS 2018 (br, clb/detail). 56 Getty Images: Kcris Ramos (cra/saffron). 57 Bridgeman Images: National Gallery, London. 58 Bridgeman Images: The Barnes Foundation, Philadelphia, Pennsylvania, USA (tl). 58-59 Bridgeman Images: The Barnes Foundation, Philadelphia, Pennsylvania, USA (c). 59 Alamy Stock Photo: James Schwabel (br). Phan Thu Trang - phanthutrang.com: (tr). 60 Bridgeman Images: Museu de Arte, Sao Paulo, Brazil (bl). 61 Photographer: Jef Aérosol: © ADAGP, Paris and DACS, London 2018 (br). akg-images: (bl). 62 Bridgeman Images: Natural History Museum, London (ca/beetle). Dorling Kindersley: Holts Gems (fclb). Getty Images: Premium UIG (tl). 63 Bridgeman Images: National Gallery, London. 64 Alamy Stock Photo: Phasin Sudjai (br). Bridgeman Images: Private Collection / Photo © Christie's Images (l). 65 Bridgeman Images: Nasjonalgalleriet, Oslo, Norway. Getty Images: Jessica Peterson (t). 66 Bridgeman Images: The Barnes Foundation, Philadelphia, Pennsylvania, USA (crb); Musée national d'Art moderne, Centre Pompidou, Paris / © ADAGP, Paris and DACS, London 2018 (tl). 67

123RF.com: bartkowski (tr). Bridgeman Images: The Israel Museum, Jerusalem, Israel / The Arthur and Madeleine Chalette Lejwa Collection (crb). Rex by Shutterstock: Geoff Caddick / EPA / © Succession Picasso / DACS, London 2018 (l). 68 Bridgeman Images: Norton Simon Museum, Pasadena, CA, USA. 69 Dreamstime.com: Fotoeye75 (tc); Paulpaladin (bl). 70-71 Hammer Museum: Henri Matisse I La Gerbe, 1953 I Gouache on paper, cut and pasted, on paper, and mounted on canvas I Object: 115 1/2 x 138 x 1 1/4 in. (293.4 x 350.5 x 3.2 cm) I Collection University of California, Los Angeles. Hammer Museum. Gift of Mr. and Mrs. Sidney F. Brody / © Succession H. Matisse / DACS 2018 (b). 71 Bridgeman Images: © Béatrice Coron (tr). 72 Photo Scala, Florence: Photothèque R. Magritte / ADAGP Images, Paris / © ADAGP, Paris and DACS, London (r). 73 © Salvador Dalí, Fundació Gala-Salvador Dalí, Figueres, 2011: © Salvador Dali, Fundació Gala-Salvador Dali, DACS 2018 (tr). The Solomon R. Guggenheim Museum, New York: Joan Miró I Figure, Dog, Birds, 1946 I Gouache and watercolor on paper I 8 ¼ x 12 ¼ inches (21 x 31.1 cm) I Solomon R. Guggenheim Museum, New York I Gift, Andrew Powie Fuller and Geraldine Spreckels Fuller Collection, 1999 I 2009.14 / © Successió Miró / ADAGP, Paris and DACS London 2018 (crb). 74 akg-images: Heritage-Images / The Print Collector (r). Bridgeman Images: National Gallery, London (l). 75 akg-images: Mondadori Portfolio / Walter Mori / Chagall ® / © ADAGP, Paris and DACS, London 2018 (main). 76 akg-images: Pictures From History. Dreamstime.com: Krzysztof Slusarczyk (fbr). 77 Bridgeman Images: Museum of Fine Arts, Houston, Texas, USA / Museum purchase funded by the Agnes Cullen Arnold Endowment Fund (tr). Dreamstime.com: Lgor Dolgov / Id1974 (clb). 78 Bridgeman Images: Haags Gemeentemuseum, The Hague, Netherlands. 79 Photo Scala, Florence: Albright Knox Art Gallery / Art Resource, NY / © The Pollock-Krasner Foundation ARS, NY and DACS, London 2018 (t, tl). 80 Alamy Stock Photo: Rweisswald / YAYOI KUSAMA (tr). Bridgeman Images: Private Collection / © 2018 The Andy Warhol Foundation for the Visual Arts, Inc. / Licensed by DACS, London (bl). 81 Bridgeman Images: Arts Council Collection, Southbank Centre, London / © Peter Blake. All rights reserved, DACS 2018 (tr); Private Collection / Photo © Christie's Image / © Wayne Thiebaud / DACS, London / VAGA, NY 2018 (tr). 82 akg-images: Heritage / Fine Art Images (t). 83 Bridgeman Images: National Gallery of Art, Washington DC (r). 84 Bridgeman Images: Musée d'art moderne de la ville de Paris, Paris / De Agostini Picture Library / G. Dagli Orti / © ADAGP, Paris and DACS, London 2018. 85 ©Tate, London 2018: Bridget Riley I Hesitate I 1964 I Emulsion on board I 106.7 × 112.4 cm I © Bridget Riley 2018. All rights reserved. (tr). 86 Getty Images: Matt McClain / The Washington Post (ca); Hannah Peters (tc). Spike Island: Lubaina Himid, Naming the Money (2004) Exhibition view, Navigation Charts (2017) Spike Island, Bristol. Courtesy the artist, Hollybush Gardens and National Museums Liverpool. Photograph courtesy Spike Island and Stuart Whipps (photographer) (crb). 86-87 Yayoi Kusama: The obliteration room 2002 to present I Furniture, white paint, dot stickers I Dimensions variable I Collaboration between Yayoi Kusama and Queensland Art Gallery. Commissioned Queensland Art Gallery, Australia. Gift of the artist through the Queensland Art Gallery Foundation 2012 I Collection: Queensland Art Gallery, Brisbane (t). 87 Bridgeman Images: © Andrew Macara / Private Collection (br). Getty Images: Jahi Chikwendiu / The Washington (t). 88 akg-images: De Agostini Picture Lib. / G. Dagli Orti (ca); Pictures From History (cb); Erich Lessing (bc). Bridgeman Images: (cl, bl); De Agostini Picture Library / G. Cigolini (tr); Hanley Museum & Art Gallery, Staffordshire, UK (br). 89 akg-images: (br); Erich Lessing (tr); Heritage-Images / The Print Collector (ca). Bridgeman Images: Louvre, Paris (bl); Musée des Beaux-Arts, Rennes, France (tl). 90 akg-images: (bl). Bridgeman Images: National Gallery of Art, Washington DC / © ADAGP, Paris and DACS (cb); Private Collection / © Salvador Dali, Fundació Gala-Salvador Dali, DACS 2018 (br); Neue Pinakothek, Munich, Germany (tr/Monet). 91 Bridgeman Images: National Galleries of Scotland, Edinburgh / © Succession H. Matisse / DACS 2018 (tr, tl); Private Collection / © 1998 Kate Rothko Prizel & Christopher Rothko ARS, NY and DACS, London (bl). Getty Images: Christopher Furlong / YAYOI KUSAMA (br).

All other images © Dorling Kindersley
For further information see: www.dkimages.com

ANSWERS Page 7 Real and unreal yes, a snail (bottom right) Page 9 Using complementary colors orange and blue; green and red Page 11 The cave of the hands most people are right-handed, and so it might be that they would have blown paint holding the hollow bone with their right hand, leaving their left hand free! Animal pictures a horse Page 15 Spot it! no, it's a real bicycle! Page 23 Spot it! silver Page 29 Steel yes (8) Page 37 *The Supper at Emmaus* by their gestures: one is about to leap from his seat, the other throws his arms wide Page 40 *The Hay Wain* A little windy, with some rain likely (dark cloud) Page 48 Spot it! self-portrait no 2 Page 51 Spot it! there's one on page 24! Page 52 Spot it! very short; morning Page 57 Spot it! the artist's first name, "Vincent," is on the side of the vase Page 59 Spot it! lots of the dots and dabs are bigger, and there aren't lots of very different colors that blend together when you stand back Page 62 Primary colors red and yellow Page 69 Color of nature lime (lime-green) Page 71 Spot it! no, they are all different! Page 73 Spot it! no—the sculptures are hovering just above the elephants! Page 75 Symbols bouquets are in *King Cophetua and the Beggar Maid* (held by the beggar maid) and *The Birthday*; a crown appears in *King Cophetua and the Beggar Maid*; oranges and a dog are in *The Arnolfini Portrait* Page 76 Spot it! in the top left corner of the painting Page 78 Spot it! red Page 87 Spot it! a piano